Founding Fathers

American history, Volume 4

Michael Johnson

Published by Harmony House Publishing, 2024.

FOUNDING FATHERS

First edition. March 23, 2024.

ISBN: 979-8224155453

Written by Michael Johnson.

Table of Contents

"To the visionaries, trailblazers, and architects of a nation built on ideals of liberty, equality, and democracy, this book is dedicated. The Founding Fathers' unwavering commitment to forging a more perfect union continues to inspire generations. May their enduring legacy serve as a beacon of hope and guidance as we navigate the complexities of the American experiment. In their honor, let us strive to uphold the principles of freedom and justice for all."

Chapter 1: Introduction to the Founding Fathers

As the 18th century dawned on the American colonies, the seeds of discontent were sown deep within the hearts and minds of its inhabitants. For generations, colonists had thrived under British rule, building communities, establishing trade networks, and cultivating the land. However, as the British Empire expanded its reach and tightened its grip on its American territories, tensions began to simmer.

Historical Context:

The journey towards revolution was not a sudden one but rather a culmination of decades of grievances and resistance against British policies. The colonies, though geographically distant from the seat of power in London, found themselves subject to increasingly burdensome taxes, trade restrictions, and infringements on their rights.

The series of events that led to the American Revolution can be traced back to the mid-18th century with the enactment of measures such as the Sugar Act (1764) and the Stamp Act (1765). These acts imposed direct taxes on the colonies without their consent, leading to widespread protests and acts of civil disobedience.

The resistance only intensified with the passage of the Townshend Acts (1767) and the Tea Act (1773), which further fueled colonial anger and resentment towards British rule. The Boston Tea Party of 1773, where colonists dumped crates of British tea into Boston Harbor in protest of the Tea Act, served as a poignant symbol of colonial defiance.

Introduction to Key Figures:

Amidst the growing unrest, a group of remarkable individuals emerged as leaders of the burgeoning independence movement. These men, known as the Founding Fathers, would play pivotal roles in shaping the destiny of the American colonies and laying the foundation for a new nation.

George Washington: Born into a prominent Virginia family in 1732, George Washington would rise to prominence as a military leader and statesman. His military prowess and leadership during the Revolutionary War earned him the title of the "Father of His Country." Washington would go on to become the first President of the United States, setting important precedents for the office and guiding the fledgling nation through its formative years.

Thomas Jefferson: A native of Virginia, Thomas Jefferson was a polymath whose intellect and vision would leave an indelible mark on American history. Jefferson is perhaps best known as the principal author of the Declaration of Independence, where he eloquently articulated the colonists' grievances against British tyranny and asserted the right to self-governance. Jefferson's contributions extended beyond the realm of politics, as he would later serve as the third President of the United States and champion the ideals of liberty, equality, and democracy.

Benjamin Franklin: A true Renaissance man, Benjamin Franklin was a scientist, inventor, philosopher, and statesman. His experiments with electricity and inventions such as the lightning rod and bifocals earned him international acclaim, while his writings on liberty and virtue helped shape the intellectual foundations of the American Revolution. Franklin played a crucial role in securing French support for the American cause during the Revolutionary War, serving as a diplomat and ambassador to France.

John Adams: A fiery advocate for independence, John Adams was a key figure in the early stages of the revolution. Adams was instrumental in drafting the Declaration of Independence and played a leading role in securing support for the cause both at home and abroad. He would later serve as the second President of the United States, where he faced numerous challenges, including tensions with France and the passage of the controversial Alien and Sedition Acts.

Others: In addition to these prominent figures, there were countless others who contributed to the cause of American independence. Figures such as James Madison, Alexander Hamilton, and Patrick Henry played crucial roles in shaping the course of events leading up to the revolution and the founding of the United States.

Setting the Stage for the Birth of a New Nation:

By the late 18th century, the stage was set for a momentous transformation. The American colonies, united by a shared sense of grievance and a desire for self-determination, had embarked on a journey towards independence that would alter the course of history.

The Declaration of Independence, signed on July 4, 1776, marked the formal break from British rule and the birth of a new nation founded on the principles of liberty, equality, and democracy. However, the road to nationhood would be fraught with challenges and uncertainties, as the fledgling United States grappled with questions of governance, sovereignty, and identity.

In the chapters that follow, we will delve deeper into the lives and legacies of the Founding Fathers, exploring their roles in shaping the American Revolution and laying the groundwork for the democratic experiment that would become the United States of America. Through their struggles and triumphs, we will gain insight into the ideals and aspirations that continue to define the American nation to this day.

Chapter 2: Seeds of Dissent

In the years leading up to the American Revolution, a series of events fueled discontent among the American colonies, igniting a flame of resistance against British rule. These early grievances, rooted in issues of taxation, representation, and individual rights, laid the groundwork for the revolutionary sentiments that would ultimately lead to independence.

Early Grievances against British Rule:

The American colonies had long enjoyed a degree of self-governance and autonomy, but as the British Empire sought to assert greater control over its colonial possessions, tensions began to rise. One of the primary sources of discontent was the lack of representation in the British Parliament, where colonists had no voice in the laws and taxes that governed their lives.

Additionally, the British government imposed a series of taxes and duties on the colonies, viewing them as a means of recouping the costs of defending and administering the vast empire. However, these measures were met with resistance from the colonists, who saw them as unjust and oppressive intrusions on their liberties.

The Stamp Act (1765):

One of the first major acts of resistance against British taxation was the Stamp Act of 1765. This legislation required that a variety of documents and printed materials in the colonies be produced on stamped paper, which was subject to a tax imposed by the British government. The act was met with widespread outrage and protests across the colonies, as colonists saw it as a direct assault on their rights and freedoms.

The Stamp Act Congress, convened in New York City in October 1765, brought together representatives from nine of the thirteen colonies to draft a unified response to the act. The congress issued a declaration asserting that only colonial assemblies had the right to impose taxes on the colonies and that the Stamp Act violated the principle of "no taxation without representation." The protests and boycotts that followed eventually led the British Parliament to repeal the Stamp Act in 1766, but the seeds of dissent had been sown.

The Boston Massacre (1770):

Tensions between the colonies and British authorities reached a boiling point on the evening of March 5, 1770, in Boston, Massachusetts. A confrontation between a group of colonists and British soldiers guarding the Customs House erupted into violence, resulting in the deaths of five colonists and the wounding of several others. The event, known as the Boston Massacre, served as a rallying cry for the colonists and further inflamed anti-British sentiment.

The Boston Massacre became a symbol of British oppression and tyranny, as colonists viewed the use of military force against unarmed civilians as evidence of the government's disregard for their rights. Propaganda and political cartoons depicting the event circulated throughout the colonies, fueling calls for resistance and retaliation against British rule.

The Tea Act and the Boston Tea Party (1773):

The passage of the Tea Act in 1773 reignited tensions between the colonies and the British government. The act granted the British East India Company a monopoly on the sale of tea in the colonies and allowed them to sell their tea directly to colonial consumers, bypassing colonial merchants and bypassing colonial taxes. While the act lowered the price of tea for consumers, it was seen as a blatant attempt by the British government to assert its authority and undercut colonial autonomy.

In protest of the Tea Act, a group of colonists disguised as Mohawk Indians boarded three British ships docked in Boston Harbor on the night of December 16, 1773. They proceeded to dump over 300 chests of tea into the harbor, in what would become known as the Boston Tea Party. The event was a bold act of defiance against British taxation and a demonstration of the colonists' willingness to resist oppressive measures.

Growing Calls for Independence:

The events of the Stamp Act crisis, the Boston Massacre, and the Boston Tea Party galvanized colonial opposition to British rule and fueled growing calls for independence. The principles of liberty, equality, and self-determination espoused by Enlightenment philosophers such as John Locke and Jean-Jacques Rousseau resonated deeply with many colonists, who saw themselves as inheritors of these ideals.

Leaders such as Samuel Adams, John Adams, and Patrick Henry emerged as vocal advocates for independence, urging their fellow colonists to break free from British tyranny and establish a new nation based on principles of democratic governance. Pamphlets, newspapers, and speeches disseminated revolutionary ideas and stoked the flames of rebellion, as colonists began to envision a future free from British oppression.

The Committees of Correspondence, established in the early 1770s to facilitate communication and coordination among the colonies, played a crucial role in organizing resistance efforts and fostering a sense of unity among the disparate colonies. These committees served as forums for exchanging information, coordinating protests, and articulating the grievances of the colonists to a wider audience.

In the years leading up to the outbreak of war in 1775, revolutionary sentiment continued to spread throughout the colonies, as more and more colonists embraced the idea of independence and self-government. The stage was set for a showdown between the colonies and the British Empire, as the seeds of dissent blossomed into full-fledged revolution.

Chapter 3: The Declaration of Independence

The Declaration of Independence stands as one of the most significant documents in human history, a testament to the enduring principles of liberty, equality, and self-determination. Drafted by Thomas Jefferson and adopted by the Continental Congress on July 4, 1776, the Declaration marked the formal break from British rule and the birth of a new nation founded on the ideals of freedom and democracy. In this chapter, we will examine the process of drafting the Declaration, the debates and deliberations that surrounded its adoption, and the profound significance of declaring independence from British rule.

Thomas Jefferson and the Drafting of the Declaration:

Thomas Jefferson, a Virginia delegate to the Continental Congress, was tasked with drafting a formal statement declaring the colonies' independence from Great Britain. Jefferson, a gifted writer and thinker, was well-suited for the task, drawing on his background in law, philosophy, and politics to craft a document that would articulate the colonists' grievances and aspirations.

Working alone in a rented room in Philadelphia, Jefferson labored over the draft of the Declaration, drawing inspiration from a variety of sources, including Enlightenment philosophers such as John Locke and Jean-Jacques Rousseau. Jefferson's draft began with a preamble affirming the natural rights of all individuals and asserting the right of the colonies to dissolve their political ties with Great Britain. It then enumerated a list of grievances against King George III and concluded with a formal declaration of independence.

Jefferson's prose was elegant and powerful, his words ringing with a sense of moral urgency and righteous indignation. His famous assertion that "all men are created equal" would become one of the defining statements of the American Revolution, encapsulating the belief that liberty and equality were the birthrights of all humanity.

Debate and Deliberation in the Continental Congress:

Once Jefferson had completed his draft, it was presented to the Continental Congress for consideration. The Congress, composed of delegates from the thirteen colonies, engaged in spirited debate and deliberation over the contents of the Declaration, with each word and phrase scrutinized and debated.

One of the most contentious issues was Jefferson's condemnation of slavery in the draft. Many Southern delegates, who relied on slave labor for their economic livelihoods, objected to language that they felt would undermine their interests. In the end, a compromise was reached, and the language condemning slavery was removed from the final version of the Declaration.

Another point of contention was the inclusion of a passage blaming King George III for the transatlantic slave trade. While many delegates recognized the moral repugnance of the slave trade, others felt that it was not directly relevant to the issue of independence from British rule. In the end, the passage was omitted from the final draft.

Despite these disagreements, the Continental Congress ultimately voted to adopt the Declaration of Independence on July 4, 1776, with twelve of the thirteen colonies voting in favor (New York abstained). The signing of the Declaration was a momentous occasion, marking the formal break from British rule and the establishment of a new nation dedicated to the principles of liberty and self-government.

The Significance of Declaring Independence:

The Declaration of Independence was more than just a symbolic gesture; it was a bold assertion of the colonists' right to govern themselves and determine their own destiny. By declaring independence from Great Britain, the colonies were asserting their sovereignty and autonomy, casting off the shackles of colonial oppression and tyranny.

The Declaration also served as a rallying cry for the colonists, inspiring them to unite in their struggle for freedom and independence. It provided a moral and philosophical justification for the revolution, articulating the principles upon which the new nation would be founded.

Furthermore, the Declaration of Independence had profound implications for the course of human history. It was a bold affirmation of the idea that governments derive their legitimacy from the consent of the governed and that individuals have certain inalienable rights that no government can take away. These principles would inspire movements for liberty and democracy around the world, shaping the course of history for centuries to come.

In declaring independence, the American colonies were taking a leap into the unknown, risking everything in pursuit of a noble ideal. But the men who signed the Declaration knew that the cause they were fighting for was worth the sacrifice, that the principles they were defending were worth any price. And so, on that fateful day in July 1776, they affixed their signatures to a document that would change the course of history and inspire generations to come.

Chapter 4: The Revolutionary War Begins

The American Revolutionary War, often referred to simply as the Revolutionary War or the War of Independence, was a pivotal moment in world history. It marked the culmination of years of simmering tensions between the American colonies and Great Britain and ultimately resulted in the birth of a new nation, the United States of America. In this chapter, we will explore the early stages of the Revolutionary War, including key battles and events, the leadership roles of figures like George Washington, and the challenges faced by the colonies in their fight for independence.

Overview of Key Battles and Events:

The Revolutionary War officially began on April 19, 1775, with the battles of Lexington and Concord in Massachusetts. British troops, acting on orders to seize colonial arms and supplies, clashed with local militia forces in the small towns of Lexington and Concord. Although the battles were relatively small in scale, they served as a spark that ignited the flames of revolution throughout the colonies.

Following the battles of Lexington and Concord, hostilities between the colonies and Great Britain escalated rapidly. In June 1775, the Battle of Bunker Hill, fought near Boston, Massachusetts, proved to be one of the bloodiest engagements of the war. Although the British ultimately emerged victorious, the battle demonstrated the determination and fighting spirit of the colonial forces.

In December 1775, General George Washington assumed command of the newly formed Continental Army, which had been assembled to coordinate the military efforts of the colonies. Washington's leadership would prove crucial in the years to come, as he worked tirelessly to train and discipline his troops and coordinate military strategy.

The following year, in June 1776, the Continental Congress adopted the Declaration of Independence, formally declaring the colonies' independence from Great Britain. The signing of the Declaration further galvanized the colonists' resolve and intensified their commitment to the cause of independence.

In August 1776, the British launched a major offensive against New York City, hoping to crush the colonial rebellion once and for all. The ensuing Battle of Long Island resulted in a decisive British victory, with Washington narrowly escaping defeat by orchestrating a daring nighttime retreat across the East River.

Despite setbacks in New York, the American cause received a much-needed boost in December 1776 with a surprise victory at the Battle of Trenton. Washington and his troops crossed the icy Delaware River on Christmas night and launched a daring attack on Hessian mercenaries encamped at Trenton, capturing nearly a thousand prisoners and boosting morale among the colonial forces.

The following year, in October 1777, the tide of the war began to turn decisively in favor of the colonies with the pivotal Battle of Saratoga. American forces under the command of General Horatio Gates dealt a crushing defeat to a British army led by General John Burgoyne, resulting in the surrender of nearly 6,000 British soldiers. The victory at Saratoga convinced France to openly support the American cause, providing crucial military and financial assistance that would prove instrumental in securing ultimate victory.

The war continued to rage on for several more years, with notable engagements such as the Battle of Monmouth (1778), the Siege of Charleston (1780), and the Battle of Yorktown (1781) ultimately leading to British surrender and the formal recognition of American independence in the Treaty of Paris (1783).

Leadership Roles of Figures Like George Washington:

One of the most enduring figures of the Revolutionary War was George Washington, who served as Commander-in-Chief of the Continental Army throughout the conflict. Washington's leadership was characterized by his steadfast determination, strategic acumen, and unwavering commitment to the cause of independence.

Washington's military career began with his appointment as a colonel in the Virginia militia during the French and Indian War. His leadership during that conflict earned him widespread praise and recognition, laying the groundwork for his future role as Commander-in-Chief.

When the Revolutionary War broke out in 1775, Washington was appointed to lead the Continental Army, despite his lack of formal military training. Over the course of the war, he would face numerous challenges, including logistical difficulties, supply shortages, and the constant threat of British invasion.

Despite these challenges, Washington proved to be a capable and resourceful commander, employing innovative tactics and strategies to outmaneuver and outwit his British adversaries. His leadership was characterized by a keen understanding of his troops' strengths and weaknesses, as well as a deep sense of duty and responsibility to his men.

Washington's ability to inspire and motivate his troops was perhaps his greatest asset as a leader. Despite the hardships of war, he remained steadfast in his commitment to the cause of independence, instilling a sense of purpose and determination in his soldiers that would carry them through the darkest days of the conflict.

Challenges Faced by the Colonies in their Fight for Independence:

The American colonies faced numerous challenges in their fight for independence, both on the battlefield and on the home front. One of the greatest challenges was the lack of a centralized government and unified military command structure. The colonies operated largely independently of one another, making coordination and cooperation difficult at times.

Another challenge was the lack of resources and manpower available to the colonial forces. The Continental Army was often poorly equipped and undermanned, lacking the training, discipline, and experience of their British counterparts. Supply shortages and logistical difficulties plagued the colonial war effort, forcing Washington to rely on guerilla tactics and hit-and-run raids to harass and weaken the enemy.

Additionally, the colonies faced internal divisions and conflicts, particularly along ethnic, religious, and ideological lines. Loyalist sympathizers, who remained loyal to the British Crown, posed a significant threat to the colonial cause, undermining efforts to rally support for independence and sowing discord within colonial communities.

Despite these challenges, the colonies were able to overcome adversity through sheer determination, resilience, and a shared commitment to the cause of liberty. The Revolutionary War was a testament to the courage and sacrifice of the men and women who fought for independence, and it laid the foundation for the birth of a new nation founded on the principles of freedom, equality, and democracy.

Chapter 5: Forging Alliances

Throughout the course of the American Revolutionary War, the fledgling United States faced formidable challenges in its struggle for independence. One of the key factors that ultimately tipped the balance in favor of the American cause was the forging of alliances with foreign powers, most notably France. In this chapter, we will explore the diplomatic efforts undertaken to secure support from foreign nations, the pivotal role played by Benjamin Franklin as a diplomat, and the importance of foreign assistance in securing victory for the American colonies.

Diplomatic Efforts to Secure Support:

From the earliest days of the Revolutionary War, American leaders recognized the importance of securing foreign assistance to bolster their chances of success against the mighty British Empire. Without a navy or a standing army capable of challenging British dominance on the battlefield, the colonies turned to diplomacy as a means of leveling the playing field.

One of the first major diplomatic overtures was made by the Continental Congress in 1776, with the adoption of the "Model Treaty," a template for future diplomatic negotiations with foreign powers. The Model Treaty outlined the terms of a potential alliance, including provisions for military support, trade agreements, and mutual defense.

In 1777, the Continental Congress dispatched a delegation to France, led by Silas Deane, Arthur Lee, and Benjamin Franklin, to seek French support for the American cause. Their mission was to secure military aid, financial assistance, and diplomatic recognition from the French government, which had long harbored a desire to weaken its rival, Great Britain.

The Role of Benjamin Franklin as a Diplomat:

Of the three members of the American delegation to France, Benjamin Franklin emerged as the most prominent and influential figure. Franklin, already well-known and respected in European intellectual circles for his scientific achievements and philosophical writings, was ideally suited for the role of diplomat.

Franklin's charm, wit, and diplomatic skill endeared him to the French court, where he quickly became a favorite of King Louis XVI and his ministers. He used his considerable influence to lobby for French support for the American cause, emphasizing the shared values of liberty and democracy that united the two nations.

In addition to his diplomatic efforts, Franklin played a crucial role in securing financial assistance for the American cause. Through his contacts in European banking circles, Franklin was able to secure loans and credit agreements that provided much-needed funding for the Continental Army and the war effort.

Perhaps most importantly, Franklin's presence in France helped to elevate the American cause in the eyes of the European public. His writings and speeches extolling the virtues of American independence and republicanism resonated with many Europeans, inspiring support and solidarity for the American cause.

The Importance of Foreign Support:

The support of foreign powers, particularly France, played a crucial role in securing victory for the American colonies in their struggle for independence. French assistance took many forms, including military aid, financial support, and diplomatic recognition, all of which were instrumental in turning the tide of the war in favor of the Americans.

One of the most significant forms of French assistance was military aid, including the provision of weapons, ammunition, and military supplies to the Continental Army. In addition, France dispatched troops, ships, and officers to fight alongside the Americans on the battlefield, helping to tip the balance in several key engagements.

Financial support from France was also essential to the American war effort. French loans and credit agreements provided the Continental Congress with the funds needed to pay for the costs of war, including the purchase of supplies, the maintenance of the army, and the payment of soldiers' wages.

Diplomatic recognition from France and other European powers helped to legitimize the American cause on the world stage, elevating the status of the fledgling United States and bolstering its credibility as a sovereign nation. The Treaty of Alliance and the Treaty of Paris, both signed with France in 1778, formalized the Franco-American alliance and laid the groundwork for future cooperation between the two nations.

In addition to military and financial support, French assistance had a psychological impact on the war effort, boosting morale among the American troops and undermining British confidence in their ability to quell the rebellion. The knowledge that the Americans had powerful allies standing behind them gave the colonists renewed hope and determination to continue the fight for independence.

In conclusion, the forging of alliances with foreign powers, particularly France, was a crucial factor in securing victory for the American colonies in their struggle for independence. Through skillful diplomacy, strategic alliances, and unwavering determination, the Americans were able to overcome the formidable challenges they faced and achieve their long-cherished dream of liberty and self-government.

Chapter 6: The Articles of Confederation

In the aftermath of the American Revolutionary War, the newly independent United States faced the daunting task of establishing a system of government capable of governing a diverse and sprawling nation. The Articles of Confederation, adopted in 1777 and ratified in 1781, represented the first attempt at creating a national government for the fledgling republic. In this chapter, we will examine the Articles of Confederation, including their strengths and weaknesses, and the challenges faced in governing the new nation during and after the Revolutionary War.

Examination of the First Attempt at a National Government:

The Articles of Confederation were drafted by the Continental Congress in 1777 in response to the need for a centralized authority to coordinate the efforts of the newly independent states. The Articles established a confederation, or league of sovereign states, with a weak central government and strong state governments.

Under the Articles, the central government consisted of a unicameral legislature known as the Congress of the Confederation, in which each state had one vote. The Congress was responsible for conducting foreign affairs, declaring war, and managing relations with Native American tribes, among other powers. However, it lacked the authority to levy taxes, regulate commerce, or enforce its decisions, relying instead on the voluntary cooperation of the states.

The Articles of Confederation also provided for a system of state sovereignty, with each state retaining its independence, freedom, and sovereignty. The central government had limited powers and was largely dependent on the goodwill and cooperation of the individual states for its authority.

Strengths and Weaknesses of the Articles of Confederation:

The Articles of Confederation had several strengths, including their ability to preserve the independence and sovereignty of the individual states. The framers of the Articles were wary of creating a strong central government that might infringe upon the rights and liberties of the states, and thus deliberately limited the powers of the national government.

Additionally, the Articles provided a framework for cooperation and coordination among the states, particularly in matters of mutual interest such as defense and foreign affairs. The central government served as a forum for resolving disputes and negotiating agreements between the states, helping to maintain peace and stability in the young republic.

However, despite these strengths, the Articles of Confederation also had significant weaknesses that undermined their effectiveness as a system of government. Perhaps the most glaring weakness was the central government's inability to levy taxes or regulate commerce. Without the power to raise revenue, the national government struggled to fund its operations and pay off the massive debts incurred during the Revolutionary War.

Another weakness of the Articles was their lack of a strong executive branch to enforce the laws and decisions of the central government. The Congress of the Confederation was essentially a legislative body, with no executive authority to implement its policies or enforce its decrees. This lack of executive leadership contributed to a sense of disunity and inefficiency within the government.

Additionally, the Articles of Confederation provided for a cumbersome system of governance, requiring a unanimous vote of all thirteen states to amend the document. This made it nearly impossible to enact meaningful reforms or address pressing issues facing the nation, as even a single dissenting state could block any proposed changes.

Challenges in Governing the New Nation:

The challenges faced in governing the new nation under the Articles of Confederation were numerous and daunting. One of the most pressing issues was the management of the national debt, which had ballooned to over $50 million by the end of the Revolutionary War. Without the power to levy taxes, the central government struggled to raise revenue to pay off its debts, leading to economic instability and fiscal uncertainty.

Another challenge was the regulation of commerce and trade between the states. Under the Articles, each state retained the authority to regulate its own commerce, leading to a patchwork of conflicting laws and regulations that hindered interstate trade and economic development. The lack of a unified trade policy also made it difficult for the United States to negotiate trade agreements with foreign nations, further hampering economic growth.

Additionally, the central government struggled to maintain order and security on the frontier, where conflicts with Native American tribes and European powers threatened the stability of the young republic. Without a standing army or the authority to raise troops, the central government relied on state militias to maintain peace and defend the nation's borders, with mixed results.

The weaknesses of the Articles of Confederation became increasingly apparent in the years following the Revolutionary War, as the central government proved unable to effectively address the pressing challenges facing the nation. Economic instability, political disunity, and social unrest threatened to unravel the fragile fabric of the new republic, leading many to question the viability of the Articles as a system of government.

In conclusion, while the Articles of Confederation represented a bold experiment in republican governance, they ultimately proved inadequate to the task of governing a rapidly expanding and increasingly complex nation. The weaknesses inherent in the Articles highlighted the need for a stronger and more centralized system of government, leading to the eventual drafting and ratification of the United States Constitution in 1787.

Chapter 7: Crafting the Constitution

The Constitutional Convention of 1787 stands as one of the most significant events in American history, as it brought together delegates from across the newly independent United States to draft a new system of government to replace the faltering Articles of Confederation. Over the course of several months, these delegates engaged in spirited debate, intense negotiation, and ultimately, hard-fought compromise to craft the United States Constitution, a document that would serve as the foundation of the American republic for centuries to come. In this chapter, we will explore the process of drafting the Constitution, the key issues addressed, and the contributions of notable figures such as James Madison, Alexander Hamilton, and others.

Debate and Compromise at the Constitutional Convention:

The Constitutional Convention convened in Philadelphia on May 25, 1787, with the stated purpose of revising the Articles of Confederation. However, it quickly became apparent to the delegates that more drastic measures were needed to address the weaknesses of the existing system of government. Over the course of several months, the delegates engaged in heated debates and negotiations, grappling with issues such as representation, federalism, and the balance of powers.

One of the most contentious issues facing the convention was the question of representation in the national legislature. Large states, such as Virginia and Pennsylvania, advocated for representation based on population, while smaller states, such as New Jersey and Delaware, argued for equal representation for all states regardless of size. The resulting deadlock threatened to derail the convention until a compromise, known as the Great Compromise, was reached. This compromise established a bicameral legislature, with representation in the House of Representatives based on population and equal representation in the Senate, with each state receiving two senators.

Another key issue addressed at the convention was the balance of powers between the federal government and the states. Some delegates, known as

Federalists, argued for a strong central government with broad powers to address the weaknesses of the Articles of Confederation. Others, known as Anti-Federalists, were wary of centralized authority and advocated for a more limited federal government with greater powers reserved for the states. The resulting compromise, embodied in the Constitution's system of federalism, struck a delicate balance between state sovereignty and federal authority.

Throughout the convention, delegates grappled with a myriad of other issues, including the separation of powers, the role of the executive branch, and the protection of individual rights. Through compromise and negotiation, they were able to draft a document that addressed these concerns while laying the groundwork for a stable and effective system of government.

Key Issues Addressed:

The delegates at the Constitutional Convention addressed a wide range of issues in drafting the United States Constitution, many of which continue to shape American politics and governance to this day. Some of the key issues addressed include:

- Representation: The question of representation in the national legislature was one of the most contentious issues facing the convention. The Great Compromise, which established a bicameral legislature with representation based on both population and equal state representation, resolved this issue.

- Federalism: The balance of powers between the federal government and the states was a central concern at the convention. The Constitution's system of federalism, which divides powers between the national and state governments, struck a delicate balance between state sovereignty and federal authority.

- Separation of Powers: The delegates sought to prevent the concentration of power in any one branch of government by dividing powers among three separate branches: the legislative, executive, and judicial branches. This system of checks and balances ensured that no branch could usurp the authority of the others.

- The Role of the Executive: The delegates debated the powers and responsibilities of the executive branch, ultimately creating a strong executive with the authority to enforce the laws, conduct foreign affairs, and serve as commander-in-chief of the armed forces.

- Protection of Individual Rights: The Bill of Rights, the first ten amendments to the Constitution, was added to address concerns about the protection of individual rights and liberties. These amendments guarantee freedoms such as freedom of speech, religion, and the press, as well as protections against unreasonable search and seizure and cruel and unusual punishment.

The Contributions of Figures Like James Madison, Alexander Hamilton, and Others:

Several key figures played instrumental roles in the drafting and ratification of the United States Constitution, including James Madison, Alexander Hamilton, and others.

James Madison, often referred to as the "Father of the Constitution," was one of the principal architects of the document. As a delegate from Virginia, Madison played a leading role in shaping the structure and content of the Constitution, particularly in his advocacy for a strong central government and the protection of individual rights. Madison's contributions to the convention, including his notes on the proceedings, provided invaluable insights into the drafting process and the debates that took place.

Alexander Hamilton, another delegate from New York, was a staunch advocate for a strong central government with broad powers to address the weaknesses of the Articles of Confederation. Hamilton played a key role in drafting the Constitution's provisions on taxation, commerce, and the executive branch, and later played a crucial role in securing ratification of the Constitution through his efforts in writing The Federalist Papers.

Other notable figures at the convention included Benjamin Franklin, George Washington, and Gouverneur Morris, each of whom made important contributions to the drafting and ratification of the Constitution. Franklin, the elder statesman of the convention, provided sage counsel and guidance to his fellow delegates, while Washington, the presiding officer of the convention, lent his considerable prestige and authority to the proceedings. Morris, a delegate from Pennsylvania, played a key role in drafting the final text of the Constitution, including its famous preamble.

In conclusion, the drafting of the United States Constitution was a monumental achievement that laid the groundwork for a stable and effective system of government. Through debate, compromise, and negotiation, the delegates at the Constitutional Convention were able to craft a document that addressed the pressing issues of their time while laying the foundation for a more perfect union. Their contributions continue to shape American politics and governance to this day, reminding us of the enduring legacy of the Constitution and the ideals it embodies.

Chapter 8: Ratification and the Bill of Rights

The ratification of the United States Constitution was a pivotal moment in American history, marking the culmination of months of debate, negotiation, and compromise at the Constitutional Convention. Yet, the journey towards ratification was far from smooth, as it sparked intense debates and fierce opposition from Anti-Federalists who feared that the proposed Constitution would threaten individual liberties and concentrate too much power in the hands of the federal government. In response to these concerns, the promise of a Bill of Rights emerged as a crucial compromise, assuaging fears about government overreach and securing support for the Constitution. In this chapter, we will delve into the ratification process, the debates over the Constitution, and the significance of the Bill of Rights in securing support for the newly drafted Constitution.

The Ratification Process and the Debates over the Constitution:

Following the conclusion of the Constitutional Convention in September 1787, the proposed Constitution was submitted to the states for ratification. The ratification process was outlined in Article VII of the Constitution, which stipulated that the document would become binding upon ratification by nine of the thirteen states. Each state convened a ratifying convention to debate the merits of the Constitution and decide whether to accept or reject it.

Almost immediately, the proposed Constitution sparked vigorous debates across the country. Supporters of the Constitution, known as Federalists, argued that it provided a necessary framework for a strong and effective central government, capable of addressing the weaknesses of the Articles of Confederation and promoting the common good. Federalist leaders such as Alexander Hamilton, James Madison, and John Jay penned a series of essays known as The Federalist Papers, which were published in newspapers across the country and made a compelling case for ratification.

However, the Constitution also faced fierce opposition from Anti-Federalists, who feared that it would threaten individual liberties and consolidate too much power in the hands of the federal government. Anti-Federalist leaders such as Patrick Henry, George Mason, and Richard Henry Lee raised concerns about the lack of a bill of rights to protect fundamental freedoms, the potential for abuse of power by the executive branch, and the erosion of state sovereignty. Anti-Federalist newspapers published scathing critiques of the proposed Constitution, warning of the dangers of tyranny and oppression.

The ratification debates were often heated and contentious, with both sides employing a variety of tactics to sway public opinion. Federalists emphasized the benefits of a strong central government and the need for national unity and stability, while Anti-Federalists warned of the dangers of unchecked power and called for greater protections for individual rights.

In the end, despite fierce opposition from Anti-Federalists in several states, the Constitution was ultimately ratified by the requisite nine states, with New Hampshire becoming the ninth state to ratify on June 21, 1788. However, the fight for ratification was far from over, as several key states, including New York and Virginia, had yet to decide whether to accept or reject the proposed Constitution.

The Promise of a Bill of Rights:

One of the most significant concessions made to Anti-Federalist concerns during the ratification debates was the promise of a Bill of Rights to protect individual liberties. Anti-Federalists argued that the Constitution lacked adequate safeguards against government overreach and insisted on the inclusion of explicit guarantees of fundamental freedoms.

In response to these concerns, James Madison, a Federalist delegate from Virginia, proposed a series of amendments to the Constitution that would address Anti-Federalist concerns and protect individual rights. Madison's proposals drew heavily on the Virginia Declaration of Rights, drafted by George Mason in 1776, which had served as a model for similar declarations adopted by other states.

Madison's proposed amendments, which would later become known as the Bill of Rights, included provisions protecting freedom of speech, religion, and the press; the right to keep and bear arms; protections against unreasonable search and seizure; and safeguards against cruel and unusual punishment. These amendments were designed to enshrine in law the principles of liberty, equality, and justice that were central to the American experiment in self-government.

The promise of a Bill of Rights proved crucial in securing support for the Constitution in several key states, including New York and Virginia, where Anti-Federalist sentiment was particularly strong. In New York, for example, the ratifying convention narrowly approved the Constitution on the condition that a Bill of Rights be added as soon as possible. Similarly, in Virginia, the promise of a Bill of Rights helped to sway opinion in favor of ratification, with Anti-Federalist leaders such as Patrick Henry ultimately endorsing the Constitution.

The Significance of the Bill of Rights:

The Bill of Rights was ratified by the states in 1791, two years after the Constitution itself had been ratified. Its adoption marked a significant milestone in American history, reaffirming the commitment of the United States to the principles of liberty, equality, and justice.

The Bill of Rights has served as a cornerstone of American democracy, providing essential protections for individual rights and liberties against government intrusion and abuse of power. Its guarantees of freedom of speech, religion, and the press have enabled Americans to speak their minds, worship as they choose, and express themselves without fear of censorship or persecution.

Similarly, the Bill of Rights has protected Americans against unreasonable searches and seizures and safeguarded their right to due process of law, ensuring that all individuals are treated fairly and justly under the legal system. The right to bear arms has become a deeply ingrained aspect of American culture and identity, while protections against cruel and unusual punishment underscore the nation's commitment to human dignity and respect for basic human rights.

Moreover, the Bill of Rights has played a crucial role in shaping the relationship between citizens and their government, serving as a constant reminder of the limitations of governmental authority and the importance of individual freedoms. Its provisions have been invoked countless times throughout American history to challenge unjust laws, defend civil liberties, and hold government officials accountable for their actions.

Furthermore, the inclusion of the Bill of Rights helped to reassure Anti-Federalists that their concerns about government overreach and individual rights had been addressed, paving the way for broader acceptance of the Constitution and fostering a spirit of unity and cooperation among the states.

In addition to its practical significance, the Bill of Rights holds immense symbolic value as a testament to the enduring principles upon which the United States was founded. It serves as a reminder of the sacrifices made by the Founding Fathers to secure the blessings of liberty for themselves and future generations, and as a beacon of hope for all who seek to live in a society governed by the rule of law and respect for human dignity.

In conclusion, the ratification of the United States Constitution and the subsequent adoption of the Bill of Rights represent defining moments in American history. The debates over the Constitution and the promise of a Bill of Rights underscored the deeply held convictions of the American people regarding the importance of individual liberties and the limits of governmental authority. By enshrining these principles in law, the Founding Fathers laid the groundwork for a more perfect union, built upon the timeless ideals of freedom, equality, and justice for all.

Chapter 9: The Federalist Era

The Federalist Era marks the early years of the newly independent United States, characterized by the leadership of George Washington, the establishment of key institutions and policies, and the emergence of political factions, most notably the Federalist Party. This period, spanning roughly from 1789 to 1801, laid the foundation for the young nation's political, economic, and social development and set the stage for its future trajectory as a global power. In this chapter, we will explore the events, policies, and personalities that defined the Federalist Era and shaped the course of American history.

1. Inauguration of George Washington:**

The Federalist Era began with the inauguration of George Washington as the nation's first president on April 30, 1789. Washington's unanimous election by the Electoral College reflected his stature as the indispensable figure of the American Revolution and his widespread popularity among the American people. In his inaugural address, Washington emphasized the need for national unity and cooperation, urging his fellow citizens to set aside sectional differences and work together for the common good.

As president, Washington faced the formidable task of building a new government from scratch and guiding the young nation through its formative years. He assembled a talented and diverse cabinet, including luminaries such as Alexander Hamilton as Secretary of the Treasury and Thomas Jefferson as Secretary of State, to help him tackle the myriad challenges facing the country.

2. Establishment of Key Institutions and Policies:

One of the most significant achievements of the Federalist Era was the establishment of key institutions and policies that laid the groundwork for the future growth and prosperity of the United States. One of Washington's first priorities as president was to establish a strong and effective central government capable of asserting its authority over the states and promoting the nation's interests both at home and abroad.

To this end, Washington and his administration worked tirelessly to implement policies aimed at strengthening the federal government and fostering economic growth. One of the most important initiatives of the Federalist Era was the establishment of the federal court system, including the Supreme Court and lower federal courts, through the Judiciary Act of 1789. This landmark legislation provided for the organization and jurisdiction of the federal judiciary, ensuring the supremacy of federal law and the protection of individual rights.

Another key policy initiative of the Federalist Era was the implementation of Hamilton's ambitious financial program. As Secretary of the Treasury, Hamilton proposed a series of measures aimed at stabilizing the nation's finances, including the assumption of state debts, the establishment of a national bank, and the imposition of tariffs and excise taxes to raise revenue. Despite fierce opposition from Jefferson and his allies, Hamilton's financial program was ultimately adopted by Congress and laid the foundation for the nation's modern financial system.

3. Emergence of Political Factions:

The Federalist Era also witnessed the emergence of political factions and the rise of organized political parties, as competing visions for the future of the nation clashed in the arena of public debate. The two dominant factions of the era were the Federalists, led by Hamilton and John Adams, and the Democratic-Republicans, led by Jefferson and James Madison.

The Federalists advocated for a strong central government, a broad interpretation of the Constitution, and policies favoring urban commercial interests and close ties with Great Britain. They believed that a strong federal government was necessary to promote economic development, maintain national security, and uphold the rule of law.

In contrast, the Democratic-Republicans favored a more limited role for the federal government, a strict interpretation of the Constitution, and policies favoring agrarian interests and close ties with France. They feared that a strong central government would encroach upon the rights and liberties of the states and the people and sought to preserve the decentralized system of government established by the Articles of Confederation.

The rivalry between the Federalists and Democratic-Republicans intensified during the Federalist Era, as competing visions for the future of the nation clashed in debates over issues such as the national bank, tariffs, and foreign policy. The partisan divide deepened as the two factions mobilized their supporters through newspapers, pamphlets, and public speeches, laying the groundwork for the emergence of organized political parties.

4. The Rise of the Federalist Party:

The Federalist Party emerged as the dominant political force of the Federalist Era, wielding significant influence over the policies and direction of the federal government. Led by Hamilton, Adams, and other prominent Federalist leaders, the party championed the principles of a strong central government, economic development, and close ties with Great Britain.

Under Hamilton's leadership, the Federalists successfully implemented their agenda of fiscal and economic reform, including the establishment of the national bank, the assumption of state debts, and the imposition of tariffs and excise taxes. These policies helped to stabilize the nation's finances, promote economic growth, and strengthen the federal government's authority.

In addition to their economic agenda, the Federalists also pursued a proactive foreign policy aimed at safeguarding American interests abroad and maintaining peace and stability in the international arena. Despite initial tensions with Great Britain and France, the Federalists ultimately favored closer ties with Great Britain, viewing it as a more reliable and stable ally.

However, the Federalist Party's dominance was not unchallenged, as opposition from the Democratic-Republicans and internal divisions within the party threatened to undermine its political influence. The XYZ Affair, a diplomatic incident involving French attempts to extort bribes from American diplomats, and the passage of the Alien and Sedition Acts, which were seen as an attack on civil liberties, eroded support for the Federalist Party and contributed to its eventual decline.

5. Legacy of the Federalist Era:

The Federalist Era left a lasting legacy that continues to shape American politics and governance to this day. The policies and institutions established during this period laid the foundation for the nation's modern system of government, including its strong central government, independent judiciary, and modern financial system.

Moreover, the emergence of political factions and the rise of organized political parties set the stage for the development of the two-party system that remains a defining feature of American politics. The rivalry between the Federalists and Democratic-Republicans established a pattern of partisan conflict and competition that has persisted throughout American history.

In conclusion, the Federalist Era was a period of profound transformation and upheaval in American history, as the young nation grappled with the challenges of building a new government and defining its place in the world. Under the leadership of George Washington and the Federalist Party, the United States laid the groundwork for its future growth and prosperity, setting the stage for its emergence as a global superpower.

Chapter 10: Jeffersonian Democracy

The Jeffersonian Democracy era marks a significant period in American history characterized by the presidency of Thomas Jefferson, the expansion of the United States through the Louisiana Purchase, and various challenges faced by the nation, including the embargo and foreign policy issues. Thomas Jefferson's presidency represented a shift in American politics and governance, as he sought to implement his vision of a decentralized agrarian republic grounded in principles of individual liberty, limited government, and states' rights. In this chapter, we will explore Jefferson's presidency, the impact of the Louisiana Purchase on American expansion, and the challenges encountered during this transformative era.

1. Thomas Jefferson's Presidency and Vision for the Nation:

Thomas Jefferson assumed the presidency of the United States on March 4, 1801, after a bitterly contested election against incumbent President John Adams. Jefferson's victory marked the first peaceful transfer of power between political parties in American history, as the Democratic-Republicans defeated the Federalist Party, signaling a shift in the nation's political landscape.

Jefferson's presidency was guided by a deeply held belief in the principles of republicanism, agrarianism, and limited government. He envisioned an America composed of independent yeoman farmers, free from the influence of entrenched elites and distant governments. Jefferson's vision of a decentralized agrarian republic stood in stark contrast to the Federalist vision of a strong central government and a commercial society.

As president, Jefferson sought to implement his vision through a series of policy initiatives aimed at reducing the size and scope of the federal government, promoting agrarian interests, and expanding individual liberties. He championed policies such as reducing the national debt, cutting government spending, and repealing the excise tax on whiskey, which he viewed as an unfair burden on rural farmers.

Jefferson also prioritized the protection of civil liberties and individual rights, championing the principles of freedom of speech, religion, and the press. He sought to limit the power of the federal government and protect states' rights, advocating for a strict interpretation of the Constitution and resisting efforts to expand federal authority beyond its enumerated powers.

2. Expansion of the United States through the Louisiana Purchase:

One of the most significant achievements of Jefferson's presidency was the acquisition of the Louisiana Territory from France through the Louisiana Purchase. In 1803, Jefferson negotiated the purchase of the vast territory, which encompassed more than 800,000 square miles of land west of the Mississippi River, from French Emperor Napoleon Bonaparte for $15 million.

The Louisiana Purchase doubled the size of the United States overnight, opening up vast new opportunities for westward expansion and economic growth. It also secured American control over the vital Mississippi River and the strategic port of New Orleans, ensuring access to the valuable trade routes of the Mississippi Valley.

The acquisition of the Louisiana Territory represented a triumph of Jefferson's vision of a continental empire of liberty, where independent farmers could settle and cultivate the land free from the constraints of aristocracy and centralized authority. It also laid the groundwork for future expansion and the fulfillment of America's manifest destiny to extend its influence from coast to coast.

3. Challenges such as the Embargo and Foreign Policy Issues:

Despite the successes of Jefferson's presidency, his administration faced numerous challenges, including the imposition of the embargo, foreign policy crises, and the threat of war with European powers.

One of the most controversial policies of Jefferson's presidency was the imposition of the Embargo Act of 1807, which sought to punish Britain and France for their violations of American neutrality by banning all trade with foreign nations. The embargo had disastrous effects on the American economy, leading to widespread unemployment, bankruptcies, and economic hardship for American merchants and farmers.

Moreover, the embargo failed to achieve its intended goals of compelling Britain and France to respect American neutrality, as both nations continued to seize American ships and impress American sailors into their service. The embargo was eventually repealed in 1809, but not before inflicting significant damage on the American economy and undermining Jefferson's popularity.

In addition to domestic challenges, Jefferson's presidency was also marked by foreign policy crises, including tensions with Britain and France over maritime rights, trade restrictions, and impressment of American sailors. The Chesapeake-Leopard Affair, in which a British warship attacked and boarded an American naval vessel, inflamed anti-British sentiment and brought the United States to the brink of war with Britain.

Similarly, Jefferson faced challenges in dealing with the Barbary pirates of North Africa, who preyed on American merchant ships and demanded tribute in exchange for safe passage through their waters. Jefferson's response to the Barbary threat was mixed, as he initially sought to negotiate a peaceful resolution but ultimately authorized a series of military actions against the pirate strongholds.

4. Legacy of Jeffersonian Democracy:

Despite the challenges encountered during Jefferson's presidency, his administration left a lasting legacy that continues to shape American politics, governance, and identity to this day. Jefferson's commitment to individual liberty, limited government, and states' rights helped to define the character of the American republic and set the stage for its future development.

The Louisiana Purchase, Jefferson's most enduring achievement, transformed the United States into a continental power and opened up vast new opportunities for westward expansion and economic growth. It also reinforced America's commitment to territorial expansion and the fulfillment of its manifest destiny to extend its influence from coast to coast.

Moreover, Jefferson's presidency laid the groundwork for the emergence of a distinctively American identity rooted in principles of republicanism, egalitarianism, and individualism. His vision of a decentralized agrarian republic, where independent farmers could thrive free from the constraints of aristocracy and centralized authority, continues to resonate with Americans today.

In conclusion, the Jeffersonian Democracy era was a period of profound transformation and upheaval in American history, as the young nation grappled with the challenges of building a new government, expanding its territory, and asserting its place on the world stage. Despite the challenges encountered during this transformative era, Jefferson's presidency left an indelible mark on the nation, shaping its political, economic, and social development for generations to come.

Chapter 11: War of 1812

The War of 1812 stands as a pivotal moment in American history, marking a significant chapter in the young nation's struggle for independence and sovereignty. Fought between the United States and Great Britain from 1812 to 1815, the conflict arose from a complex web of political, economic, and territorial disputes, and its consequences reverberated far beyond the battlefield. In this chapter, we will delve into the causes and consequences of the War of 1812, examine the leadership during the conflict, including figures like James Madison and Andrew Jackson, and explore its impact on the nation's identity and relationships with foreign powers.

1. Causes of the War of 1812:

The War of 1812 was driven by a combination of long-standing grievances and immediate provocations that ultimately pushed the United States and Great Britain to the brink of war. Several key factors contributed to the outbreak of hostilities, including:

a. Maritime Issues: One of the primary causes of the War of 1812 was the ongoing maritime disputes between the United States and Great Britain. British naval policies, such as impressment, the practice of seizing American sailors and forcing them to serve in the Royal Navy, deeply angered the American public and fueled anti-British sentiment. Additionally, British interference with American shipping and trade, including the seizure of American ships and goods, further strained relations between the two nations.

b. Territorial Disputes: Territorial tensions also played a significant role in triggering the war. The United States sought to expand its territory westward, but Great Britain, which still maintained control over several territories in North America, including Canada, actively opposed American expansion. Additionally, Native American tribes in the Northwest Territory, with British support, resisted American encroachment on their lands, leading to conflict along the frontier.

c. Impressment and Trade Restrictions: British policies of impressment and trade restrictions, such as the Orders in Council, which restricted American trade with France, exacerbated tensions between the United States and Great

Britain. These policies were seen as violations of American sovereignty and economic interests and contributed to growing calls for war among American policymakers and the public.

2. Consequences of the War of 1812:

The War of 1812 had far-reaching consequences for both the United States and Great Britain, shaping the course of North American history and influencing the geopolitical landscape for decades to come. Some of the key consequences of the war include:

a. National Identity: The War of 1812 played a crucial role in shaping the national identity of the United States, solidifying its status as an independent and sovereign nation. The successful defense of American territory against British invasion and the heroic exploits of American military leaders such as Andrew Jackson and Oliver Hazard Perry helped to foster a sense of national pride and unity among Americans.

b. Expansion of American Territory: Despite the mixed outcomes of the war, the conflict ultimately resulted in the expansion of American territory and influence. The Treaty of Ghent, which ended the war in 1815, affirmed the status quo antebellum, returning all captured territory to its pre-war owners and failing to address the underlying issues that had led to the conflict. However, the war effectively ended British support for Native American resistance to American expansion, paving the way for further westward expansion.

c. Weakening of Native American Resistance: The War of 1812 dealt a significant blow to Native American resistance to American expansion in the Northwest Territory. With British support diminished and American military victories on the frontier, Native American tribes such as the Shawnee and the Creek were forced to cede large tracts of land to the United States in subsequent treaties, accelerating the process of westward expansion.

d. Rise of American Nationalism: The War of 1812 also contributed to the rise of American nationalism, as the conflict brought Americans together in defense of their country and its interests. The successful defense of American territory against British invasion, coupled with victories such as the Battle of New Orleans, bolstered American confidence and pride in their nation's capabilities.

3. Leadership During the Conflict:

The War of 1812 was marked by the leadership of several key figures who played instrumental roles in guiding the United States through the conflict. Among the most prominent leaders during the war were:

a. James Madison: As the fourth president of the United States, James Madison played a central role in leading the nation through the War of 1812. Despite initial reluctance to go to war, Madison ultimately acceded to pressure from Congress and the public and declared war on Great Britain in June 1812. Madison's leadership during the conflict was characterized by his steadfast commitment to defending American interests and sovereignty, even in the face of significant challenges and setbacks.

b. Andrew Jackson: Andrew Jackson emerged as one of the most prominent military leaders of the War of 1812, achieving fame and renown for his victories at the Battle of New Orleans and elsewhere. Jackson's leadership during the war cemented his reputation as a national hero and propelled him to prominence in American politics. His decisive victory at New Orleans, which occurred after the signing of the Treaty of Ghent but before news of the treaty reached the United States, helped to restore American morale and confidence in the wake of the conflict.

c. Oliver Hazard Perry: Oliver Hazard Perry was another key military leader who distinguished himself during the War of 1812. As commander of the United States Navy's naval forces on Lake Erie, Perry achieved a decisive victory over the British Royal Navy at the Battle of Lake Erie in September 1813, capturing the entire British fleet and securing American control of the Great Lakes region. Perry's victory played a crucial role in turning the tide of the war in favor of the United States and bolstering American morale.

4. Impact on the Nation's Identity and Relationships with Foreign Powers: The War of 1812 had a profound impact on the nation's identity and its relationships with foreign powers, shaping the course of American history and influencing its interactions with the rest of the world. Some of the key impacts of the war include:

a. Strengthening of American Identity: The War of 1812 played a crucial role in strengthening American national identity and unity, solidifying the nation's status as an independent and sovereign nation. The successful defense of

American territory against British invasion and the heroic exploits of American military leaders helped to foster a sense of pride and patriotism among Americans.

b. Resurgence of American Confidence: Despite the mixed outcomes of the war, the conflict ultimately bolstered American confidence in its military capabilities and its ability to defend its interests against foreign powers. The successful defense of American territory against British invasion, coupled with victories such as the Battle of New Orleans, helped to restore American morale and confidence in the wake of the conflict.

c. Strained Relations with Great Britain: The War of 1812 strained relations between the United States and Great Britain and left a legacy of bitterness and distrust that persisted for years after the conflict. Although the Treaty of Ghent restored peace between the two nations, it failed to address the underlying issues that had led to the war, and tensions between the United States and Great Britain continued to simmer in the years that followed.

d. Expansion of American Influence: Despite the challenges and setbacks of the war, the conflict ultimately contributed to the expansion of American influence and power on the world stage. The successful defense of American territory against British invasion, coupled with victories such as the Battle of New Orleans, helped to bolster America's reputation as a capable military power. The war also demonstrated to foreign powers, particularly in Europe, that the United States was a force to be reckoned with and could defend its interests against even the mightiest nations.

e. Native American Relations: The War of 1812 had significant implications for Native American tribes, particularly those in the Northwest Territory who had aligned themselves with the British against American expansion. With British support diminished and American victories on the frontier, Native American resistance to American expansion was weakened. The subsequent treaties and land cessions forced upon Native American tribes further marginalized their role in shaping the future of the continent, leading to further displacement and dispossession.

f. Impact on Trade and Economy: The War of 1812 had profound effects on American trade and the economy. The British blockade of American ports and the disruption of trade routes caused significant economic hardship for American merchants and farmers, leading to widespread unemployment and financial distress. However, the war also spurred domestic manufacturing and industry as Americans sought to become more self-sufficient in the face of British trade restrictions.

g. Legacy of the War of 1812: The War of 1812 left a lasting legacy that continues to shape American history and identity to this day. The conflict demonstrated the resilience and determination of the American people in the face of adversity and reinforced the nation's commitment to defending its independence and sovereignty. It also helped to solidify the United States' position as a major player on the world stage and set the stage for its future growth and expansion.

In conclusion, the War of 1812 was a transformative moment in American history, marking a crucial chapter in the young nation's struggle for independence and sovereignty. Fought against the backdrop of maritime disputes, territorial tensions, and diplomatic provocations, the war tested the resolve and resilience of the American people and ultimately helped to shape the course of North American history. From the leadership of figures like James Madison and Andrew Jackson to the consequences for the nation's identity and relationships with foreign powers, the War of 1812 left an indelible mark on the American psyche and continues to influence the nation's trajectory to this day.

Chapter 12: The Era of Good Feelings

The Era of Good Feelings, spanning roughly from 1815 to 1825, was a period of relative peace, prosperity, and national unity in the United States following the War of 1812. This era was characterized by economic growth, westward expansion, and a sense of optimism and confidence in the nation's future. However, beneath the surface of this apparent unity, tensions simmered over issues such as slavery, states' rights, and the role of the federal government, foreshadowing the conflicts that would shape American politics and society in the years to come. In this chapter, we will explore the key features of the Era of Good Feelings, its impact on American society and politics, and the emerging tensions that would ultimately lead to the fracturing of this period of national unity.

1. Context:

The Era of Good Feelings emerged in the aftermath of the War of 1812, a conflict that had tested the resilience of the young nation and reaffirmed its commitment to independence and sovereignty. With the war concluded and foreign threats diminished, Americans turned their attention to domestic concerns and opportunities for growth and expansion. The Treaty of Ghent, which ended the war in 1815, restored peace between the United States and Great Britain and allowed the nation to focus on rebuilding and developing its economy and society.

2. Economic Growth and Westward Expansion:

One of the hallmarks of the Era of Good Feelings was the rapid economic growth and westward expansion that characterized this period. The United States experienced a surge in industrialization, trade, and commerce, fueled by technological advancements, government policies, and an influx of immigrants seeking opportunity in the new republic.

a. Industrialization: The period saw the rise of American industry, particularly in the Northeast, where factories sprang up to produce textiles, machinery, and other goods. Innovations such as the cotton gin, developed by Eli Whitney in 1793, revolutionized the production of cotton and spurred the growth of the cotton industry in the South. Additionally, the construction of canals and roads, such as the Erie Canal and the National Road, facilitated the movement of goods and people across the country, further stimulating economic growth.

b. Trade and Commerce: The Era of Good Feelings also witnessed a boom in international trade and commerce, as American merchants sought new markets for their goods and expanded their reach beyond the borders of the United States. The signing of trade agreements with European nations, such as the Treaty of 1815 with Britain, opened up new opportunities for American exporters and helped to fuel economic growth.

c. Westward Expansion: Perhaps the most significant aspect of the Era of Good Feelings was the rapid expansion of the United States westward. Encouraged by government policies such as the Louisiana Purchase and the opening of new territories for settlement, Americans ventured into the western frontier in search of land, opportunity, and adventure. The Louisiana Purchase of 1803, which doubled the size of the United States, provided vast new territories for settlement and laid the groundwork for the nation's westward expansion.

3. Unity and National Identity:

The Era of Good Feelings was also characterized by a sense of unity and national identity among Americans, as the nation emerged from the crucible of war and asserted its place on the world stage. The successful defense of American territory during the War of 1812, coupled with economic growth and westward expansion, fostered a sense of confidence and pride in the young republic and its accomplishments. Americans increasingly identified with their nation and its symbols, such as the flag and the Constitution, and celebrated their shared heritage and values.

4. Emerging Tensions:

However, beneath the surface of this apparent unity, tensions simmered over issues such as slavery, states' rights, and the role of the federal government, foreshadowing the conflicts that would shape American politics and society in the years to come.

a. Slavery: One of the most divisive issues of the Era of Good Feelings was the institution of slavery and its expansion into new territories acquired through westward expansion. The rapid growth of the cotton industry in the South, fueled by the demand for cotton in Northern textile mills and European markets, led to an increased demand for slave labor and intensified debates over the morality and legality of slavery. The Missouri Compromise of 1820, which admitted Missouri to the Union as a slave state and Maine as a free state, temporarily resolved the issue of slavery in the territories but did little to address the underlying tensions between North and South.

b. States' Rights: Another source of tension during the Era of Good Feelings was the question of states' rights and the scope of federal power. While many Americans celebrated the expansion of the federal government's authority in areas such as economic regulation and infrastructure development, others expressed concerns about the potential for government overreach and infringement on states' rights. The debate over the Bank of the United States, which was established in 1816 to regulate the nation's currency and promote economic stability, highlighted these tensions, as critics argued that the bank represented an unconstitutional exercise of federal power.

c. Sectionalism: The Era of Good Feelings also saw the emergence of growing sectional tensions between the North and the South, as economic, social, and political differences between the two regions became increasingly pronounced. The industrialization of the North and the expansion of the cotton industry in the South created divergent economic interests and fueled debates over tariffs, trade, and internal improvements. Additionally, cultural and social differences, such as attitudes towards slavery and the role of government, further exacerbated sectional divisions and contributed to the erosion of national unity.

5. Leadership and Political Developments:

Despite these emerging tensions, the Era of Good Feelings was also characterized by a period of political dominance by the Democratic-Republican Party and its leaders, particularly James Monroe, who served as president from 1817 to 1825. Monroe's presidency was marked by a spirit of bipartisanship and consensus-building, as he sought to heal the divisions that had arisen during the early years of the republic.

Monroe's administration was also notable for its promotion of national unity and economic development. His administration pursued policies aimed at fostering economic growth, including protective tariffs to promote domestic industry and the promotion of internal improvements such as roads and canals to facilitate commerce and transportation.

However, Monroe's presidency was not without its challenges. The emergence of sectional tensions over issues such as slavery and states' rights posed significant challenges to national unity and tested the ability of the federal government to maintain order and stability. Additionally, the Panic of 1819, a severe economic downturn caused by a speculative bubble in land and commodities markets, threatened to undermine the nation's economic stability and prosperity.

6. Legacy of the Era of Good Feelings:

The Era of Good Feelings left a complex and multifaceted legacy that continues to shape American politics and society to this day. On the one hand, it was a period of relative peace, prosperity, and national unity, characterized by economic growth, westward expansion, and a sense of optimism and confidence in the nation's future. Americans celebrated their shared heritage and values and embraced the symbols of their nationhood, fostering a sense of pride and identity as citizens of the United States.

On the other hand, the era was also marked by emerging tensions and divisions over issues such as slavery, states' rights, and the role of the federal government. These tensions would ultimately erupt into open conflict during the decades that followed, leading to the Civil War and the profound transformation of American society and politics.

In conclusion, the Era of Good Feelings was a complex and contradictory period in American history, characterized by both unity and division, optimism and uncertainty. It was a time of rapid change and transformation, as the United States emerged from the crucible of war and asserted its place on the world stage. However, beneath the surface of this apparent unity, tensions simmered over issues that would ultimately shape the course of American history for generations to come.

Chapter 13: The Monroe Doctrine

The Monroe Doctrine, articulated by President James Monroe in 1823, stands as one of the most significant foreign policy doctrines in American history. It represented a bold assertion of American influence in the Western Hemisphere and a declaration of opposition to European intervention in the affairs of the newly independent nations of Latin America. The Monroe Doctrine profoundly influenced international relations and the balance of power, shaping the course of American diplomacy and the geopolitical landscape for decades to come. In this chapter, we will explore the origins, principles, and impact of the Monroe Doctrine, examining its role in shaping American foreign policy and its enduring legacy in the modern world.

1. Origins of the Monroe Doctrine:

The Monroe Doctrine emerged in response to a confluence of events and developments in the early 19th century that threatened American interests and security. Throughout the early 1800s, the newly independent nations of Latin America were struggling to establish stable governments and secure their sovereignty in the face of European interference and intervention. Spain and other European powers sought to maintain control over their former colonies in the Americas, leading to conflicts and instability in the region.

Meanwhile, in Europe, the Congress of Vienna in 1815 sought to restore the balance of power and establish a new order following the Napoleonic Wars. European powers, particularly France and Spain, eyed the Americas as potential sources of wealth and strategic advantage, leading to fears in the United States that they might seek to reassert colonial control over the region.

In this context, President James Monroe and his Secretary of State, John Quincy Adams, recognized the need for a clear and assertive statement of American policy regarding European intervention in the Western Hemisphere. The Monroe Doctrine was born out of this recognition, as Monroe sought to protect American interests and secure the independence of the newly established nations of Latin America.

2. Principles of the Monroe Doctrine:

The Monroe Doctrine, as articulated in Monroe's annual message to Congress on December 2, 1823, consisted of several key principles that would come to define American foreign policy in the Western Hemisphere:

a. Non-Interference: The Monroe Doctrine declared that the United States would not interfere in the internal affairs of European nations or their colonies, but it also asserted that European powers should refrain from interfering in the affairs of the independent nations of the Americas.

b. Non-Colonization: The doctrine stated that the Western Hemisphere was closed to further colonization by European powers. This principle aimed to prevent European expansion into the Americas and protect the sovereignty of the newly independent nations in the region.

c. Non-Intervention: The Monroe Doctrine warned European powers against attempting to establish new colonies or extend their influence in the Western Hemisphere. It asserted that any attempt to do so would be viewed by the United States as a threat to its own security and would prompt American intervention.

d. Mutual Respect: The doctrine emphasized the mutual respect between the United States and European powers, calling for peaceful relations and cooperation based on respect for each other's sovereignty and territorial integrity.

3. Impact on International Relations:

The Monroe Doctrine had a profound impact on international relations and the balance of power, shaping the course of American diplomacy and influencing the geopolitical landscape for decades to come.

a. Asserting American Influence: The Monroe Doctrine represented a bold assertion of American influence in the Western Hemisphere and signaled to European powers that the United States would not tolerate further interference or intervention in the affairs of the newly independent nations of Latin America. By asserting its authority in the region, the United States sought to protect its own security and advance its own interests while also promoting the principles of self-determination and sovereignty.

b. Limiting European Expansion: The Monroe Doctrine served to limit European expansionism in the Western Hemisphere and protect the sovereignty of the newly independent nations of Latin America. By declaring the Americas off-limits to further colonization and intervention, the United States sought to prevent European powers from establishing new colonies or extending their influence into the region. This helped to preserve the balance of power and prevent potential conflicts between European powers in the Americas.

c. Impact on European Diplomacy: The Monroe Doctrine also influenced European diplomacy and strategic calculations, as European powers took note of America's growing assertiveness and its willingness to defend its interests in the Western Hemisphere. While some European powers initially dismissed the doctrine as empty rhetoric, they soon came to recognize its significance and adjust their policies accordingly. The doctrine served as a warning to European powers that any attempt to challenge American interests in the Americas would be met with resistance.

d. Consolidation of American Hegemony: The Monroe Doctrine contributed to the consolidation of American hegemony in the Western Hemisphere and laid the groundwork for the United States' emergence as a dominant power in the region. By asserting its authority and promoting the principles of non-interference and non-colonization, the United States sought to establish itself as the preeminent power in the Americas, exerting influence over the political, economic, and strategic affairs of the region.

4. Legacy of the Monroe Doctrine:

The Monroe Doctrine left a lasting legacy that continues to shape American foreign policy and international relations to this day. Its principles have been invoked by successive administrations as a cornerstone of American diplomacy and a guiding principle in the nation's interactions with other countries.

a. Expansion of American Influence: The Monroe Doctrine helped to expand American influence in the Western Hemisphere and establish the United States as a dominant power in the region. By asserting its authority and promoting the principles of non-interference and non-colonization, the United States sought to shape the political, economic, and strategic landscape of the Americas in accordance with its own interests.

b. Promotion of Democracy and Self-Determination: The Monroe Doctrine was grounded in principles of democracy and self-determination, as it sought to protect the sovereignty and independence of the newly established nations of Latin America. By warning European powers against interfering in the affairs of these nations, the United States sought to promote the spread of democracy and the principles of freedom and independence throughout the Western Hemisphere.

c. Defense of National Security: The Monroe Doctrine served as a defense of American national security interests, as it sought to prevent European powers from establishing colonies or military bases in the Western Hemisphere that could threaten American territory or interests. By asserting its authority in the region, the United States sought to protect its own security and advance its own interests while also promoting stability and peace in the Americas.

d. Controversies and Criticisms: Despite its enduring significance, the Monroe Doctrine has also been the subject of controversy and criticism. Some critics argue that it represented a form of American imperialism and interventionism, as it sought to assert American influence over the affairs of other nations in the Western Hemisphere. Others argue that it was hypocritical, as it claimed to promote the principles of non-interference and non-colonization while also asserting American hegemony over the region.

In conclusion, the Monroe Doctrine stands as a landmark in American foreign policy and a defining moment in the nation's history. It represented a bold assertion of American influence in the Western Hemisphere and a declaration of opposition to European intervention in the affairs of the newly independent nations of Latin America. The doctrine profoundly influenced international relations and the balance of power, shaping the course of American diplomacy and the geopolitical landscape for decades to come. Its principles continue to resonate in American foreign policy today, as the United States seeks to promote democracy, freedom, and stability in the Western Hemisphere and beyond.

Chapter 14: Legacy of the Founding Fathers

The legacy of the Founding Fathers looms large over American politics, society, and culture, casting a long shadow that continues to shape the nation's identity and trajectory. From the principles enshrined in the Declaration of Independence and the Constitution to the institutions they established and the ideals they espoused, the Founding Fathers played a central role in laying the foundation of the United States and shaping its destiny. In this chapter, we will examine the lasting impact of the Founding Fathers on American politics, society, and culture, assess their achievements and shortcomings, and explore their continuing relevance in contemporary debates and discussions.

1. Principles and Ideals:

The Founding Fathers articulated a set of principles and ideals that continue to serve as the bedrock of American democracy and governance. Chief among these principles are:

a. Republicanism: The Founding Fathers sought to establish a republican form of government, grounded in the principles of popular sovereignty, limited government, and the rule of law. They envisioned a government of, by, and for the people, with elected representatives accountable to their constituents.

b. Liberty and Individual Rights: The Founding Fathers championed the cause of liberty and individual rights, recognizing that freedom was the birthright of all humanity. They enshrined these principles in the Declaration of Independence and the Bill of Rights, which guarantee fundamental freedoms such as freedom of speech, religion, and assembly.

c. Federalism: The Founding Fathers devised a system of federalism that divided power between the national government and the states, seeking to strike a balance between centralized authority and state sovereignty. This division of powers remains a defining feature of the American political system.

2. Achievements and Shortcomings:

While the Founding Fathers achieved much in their efforts to establish a new nation, they were not without their shortcomings and contradictions. Some of their key achievements and shortcomings include:

a. Achievements:

- ***Declaration of Independence:*** The Declaration of Independence, penned by Thomas Jefferson in 1776, remains one of the most influential documents in human history. It articulated the principles of self-evident truths, unalienable rights, and the right to alter or abolish oppressive governments, inspiring generations of Americans and freedom fighters around the world.

- ***Constitutional Convention***: The Constitutional Convention of 1787, attended by such luminaries as James Madison, Alexander Hamilton, and Benjamin Franklin, resulted in the drafting of the United States Constitution. This seminal document established the framework for the federal government and remains the supreme law of the land, providing the blueprint for American democracy.

- ***Bill of Rights***: The inclusion of the Bill of Rights, the first ten amendments to the Constitution, was a significant achievement of the Founding Fathers. These amendments guarantee essential civil liberties and protections against government overreach, ensuring the rights of individuals and minority groups.

b. Shortcomings:

- ***Slavery***: Perhaps the most glaring contradiction in the legacy of the Founding Fathers is their failure to fully reckon with the institution of slavery. Many of the Founding Fathers, including George Washington, Thomas Jefferson, and James Madison, were slave owners themselves, and the Constitution accommodated and perpetuated the institution of slavery.

- ***Treatment of Native Americans***: The Founding Fathers' treatment of Native Americans is another dark stain on their legacy. Through policies of forced removal, land seizure, and broken treaties, the United States government perpetrated grave injustices against indigenous peoples, leading to displacement, dispossession, and cultural genocide.

- ***Limited Suffrage***: The Founding Fathers' conception of democracy was limited in its inclusivity, as suffrage was initially restricted to white male property owners. Women, African Americans, Native Americans, and other marginalized groups were excluded from full participation in the political process, undermining the democratic ideals espoused by the Founders.

3. Continuing Relevance:

Despite their imperfections, the Founding Fathers remain figures of immense significance and influence in American political culture. Their ideas, principles, and debates continue to inform contemporary debates and discussions, shaping the course of American politics and governance.

a. Constitutional Interpretation: The Founding Fathers' original intent and the principles they articulated continue to guide constitutional interpretation and judicial decision-making. Debates over the meaning of the Constitution, the scope of federal power, and the protection of individual rights often harken back to the intentions of the Founders and the debates of the Constitutional Convention.

b. Role of Government: The Founding Fathers' vision of limited government and individual liberty remains central to contemporary debates over the role of government in society. Advocates of limited government and states' rights often invoke the principles of the Founders to justify their positions, while proponents of a more expansive role for government emphasize the need for collective action to address pressing social and economic challenges.

c. National Identity: The Founding Fathers continue to shape America's national identity and self-image, as their achievements and ideals are celebrated and commemorated in popular culture, education, and civic life. Their statues and monuments adorn public spaces across the country, serving as reminders of their enduring influence and legacy.

d. Challenges to the Founders' Legacy: The legacy of the Founding Fathers is not without its critics, who challenge their status as heroic figures and question the relevance of their ideas in the modern world. Critics argue that the Founders' emphasis on limited government and individual liberty has failed to address systemic inequalities and injustices, leading to calls for a reevaluation of their legacy and a reassessment of America's founding principles.

In conclusion, the legacy of the Founding Fathers is a complex and multifaceted one, encompassing both their achievements and their shortcomings. While their ideas and principles continue to shape American politics, society, and culture, they are also subject to scrutiny and debate as the nation grapples with its past and charts its future course. The Founding Fathers remain figures of immense significance and influence in American history, their ideals and principles serving as touchstones in the ongoing quest for a more perfect union.

Chapter 15: Conclusion: The Evolution of the American Experiment

As we come to the conclusion of our exploration into the founding of the United States and the enduring legacy of its founders, it is essential to reflect on the remarkable journey from colonial rebellion to the establishment of a new nation. The American experiment, born out of a desire for freedom, self-determination, and democratic governance, has been marked by triumphs and tribulations, challenges and achievements. In this final chapter, we will reflect on the evolution of the American experiment, the challenges faced and lessons learned along the way, and the ongoing pursuit of liberty, equality, and democracy in the United States.

1. Colonial Rebellion and the Birth of a Nation:

The journey of the United States began with a bold act of defiance against colonial rule, as American colonists rose up against British tyranny and asserted their right to independence. The Declaration of Independence, penned by Thomas Jefferson in 1776, articulated the principles of self-evident truths, unalienable rights, and the right to alter or abolish oppressive governments. It marked the birth of a new nation founded on the ideals of liberty, equality, and democracy.

The American Revolution, fought from 1775 to 1783, was a struggle for freedom and self-governance, as colonists fought to break free from British rule and establish a government of, by, and for the people. The victory of the American patriots over the British Empire was a triumph of the human spirit and a testament to the power of perseverance, sacrifice, and determination.

2. Challenges Faced and Lessons Learned:

The journey from colonial rebellion to the establishment of a new nation was fraught with challenges and obstacles, as Americans grappled with the complexities of nation-building and governance. Some of the key challenges faced and lessons learned along the way include:

a. Nation-Building: The founding fathers faced the daunting task of building a nation from the ground up, establishing institutions, laws, and traditions that would govern the fledgling republic. They navigated debates over federalism, representation, and the balance of powers, seeking to strike a delicate balance between centralized authority and state sovereignty.

b. Slavery and Civil Rights: One of the most profound challenges faced by the founders was the institution of slavery and its legacy of oppression and injustice. Despite their commitment to liberty and equality, many of the founding fathers were slave owners themselves, and the Constitution accommodated and perpetuated the institution of slavery. The struggle for civil rights and racial equality would continue to shape American society and politics in the centuries that followed.

c. Expansion and Westward Expansion: The westward expansion of the United States posed new challenges and opportunities for the young republic, as Americans ventured into the frontier in search of land, opportunity, and adventure. The expansion of American territory raised questions about sovereignty, territorial integrity, and the rights of indigenous peoples, leading to conflicts and controversies that would shape the course of American history.

d. Economic Growth and Industrialization: The industrialization of the United States in the 19th century brought unprecedented economic growth and prosperity, but it also brought new challenges and inequalities. The rise of industry and commerce transformed American society, creating new opportunities for innovation and entrepreneurship but also exacerbating social and economic disparities.

3. The Ongoing Pursuit of Liberty, Equality, and Democracy:

Despite the challenges faced and the imperfections of its founding, the United States has remained committed to the ideals of liberty, equality, and democracy. The American experiment is an ongoing journey, characterized by a relentless pursuit of justice, progress, and human dignity.

a. Civil Rights Movement: Throughout its history, the United States has been shaped by movements for social justice and civil rights, as Americans have fought to expand the promise of liberty and equality to all citizens. From the abolitionist movement to the civil rights movement of the 20th century, Americans have challenged injustice and discrimination, seeking to create a more perfect union.

b. Democratic Governance: The United States has also remained committed to the principles of democratic governance, as Americans have sought to ensure that government of, by, and for the people endures. Despite the challenges of partisanship, polarization, and political gridlock, the United States continues to uphold the principles of democracy, with free and fair elections, respect for the rule of law, and a vibrant civic culture.

c. Global Leadership: As a beacon of freedom and democracy, the United States has played a leading role on the world stage, championing human rights, democracy, and the rule of law. From the Marshall Plan to the fight against authoritarianism and extremism, America has sought to promote peace, stability, and prosperity around the world, advancing the cause of liberty and justice for all.

4. Conclusion:

In conclusion, the evolution of the American experiment is a testament to the resilience, adaptability, and enduring spirit of the American people. From colonial rebellion to the establishment of a new nation, from the struggles for civil rights to the ongoing pursuit of liberty, equality, and democracy, the United States has faced challenges with courage and determination, always striving to live up to its founding ideals and aspirations. As we look to the future, let us remember the lessons of the past and rededicate ourselves to the noble cause of building a more just, inclusive, and democratic society for all.

Don't miss out!

Visit the website below and you can sign up to receive emails whenever Michael Johnson publishes a new book. There's no charge and no obligation.

https://books2read.com/r/B-A-OREFB-XJXZC

Did you love *Founding Fathers*? Then you should read *American Chronicles*[1] by Michael Johnson!

"American Chronicles: A History of the United States" offers a comprehensive journey through the pivotal moments that shaped the nation. From the rich tapestry of indigenous civilizations to the tumultuous struggles of the Civil Rights Movement and beyond, this book explores the key events, figures, and themes that define American history. From the Revolutionary War to the Cold War and beyond, witness the rise of a nation, the trials of war, and the ongoing quest for equality and freedom. Experience the story of America, from its origins to its enduring legacy in the modern world.

---

1. https://books2read.com/u/3y9qLL

2. https://books2read.com/u/3y9qLL

About the Author

Michael Johnson is a distinguished historian specializing in American history. With a degree in History from Harvard University, Johnson's work delves into pivotal moments, figures, and themes shaping the United States. He has authored numerous acclaimed books, offering insightful perspectives and engaging narratives. Johnson's commitment to meticulous scholarship and compelling storytelling has earned him widespread acclaim in the field. Passionate about sharing his expertise, he frequently engages in lectures and public events to foster a deeper appreciation for America's past.